WITHDRAWN

ELEPHANTS

CONTENTS

| Introduction | 4 |
| Elephant distribution | 6 |

The decline of the elephants
The slaughter	8
The ivory trade	10
Habitat destruction	12

Saving the elephant
Anti-poaching	14
Research	16
Space to survive	18
Stop the trade	20
Elephants in captivity	22
The future	24

| Elephant fact files | 26-31 |
| Index | 32 |

© Aladdin Books Ltd 1989

*First published in
the United States in 1990 by*
Gloucester Press
387 Park Avenue South
New York NY 10016

Design Rob Hillier, Andy Wilkinson
Editor Fiona Robertson
Photo Research Cecilia Weston-Baker
Illustrations Ron Hayward Associates

Printed in Belgium

All rights reserved

Library of Congress Cataloging-in-Publication Data

Bright, Michael
    Elephants/Michael Bright
      p. cm -- (Project Wildlife)
      Summary: Examines the physical characteristics, behavior and life cycle of elephants and describes their relationship with humans.
    ISBN 0-531-17215-5
    1. Elephants--Juvenile literature. [1. Elephants.] I. Title. II Series
QL737.P98B75 1990
599.6'1--dc20   89-25757 CIP A

PROJECT WILDLIFE

ELEPHANTS

Michael Bright

Gloucester Press
New York : London : Toronto : Sydney

The noble and powerful African elephant.

Introduction

The elephant is the largest living land animal, and one of the most endangered. Millions of years ago there were many species of elephants and mammoths, and they lived on all the continents. Today, just two species survive – the African and the Asian – and they, too, are on the path that leads to extinction. Elephants are killed mainly for their pair of elongated incisor teeth – the tusks. These are sold as ivory. Since ancient times there has been a trade in ivory and it has always, like gold, been considered valuable. Wealthy people have always bought and kept ivory as a means of investing their wealth. Traditionally, tribal hunters, like those in East Africa, have taken elephants for their meat and ivory, and the trade had little impact on the elephant population. Then, in the early 1970s, the value of currencies collapsed and people began to buy as much gold and ivory as they could, knowing they would retain their value. Suddenly, the price of ivory soared and elephants were slaughtered. The killing continues today.

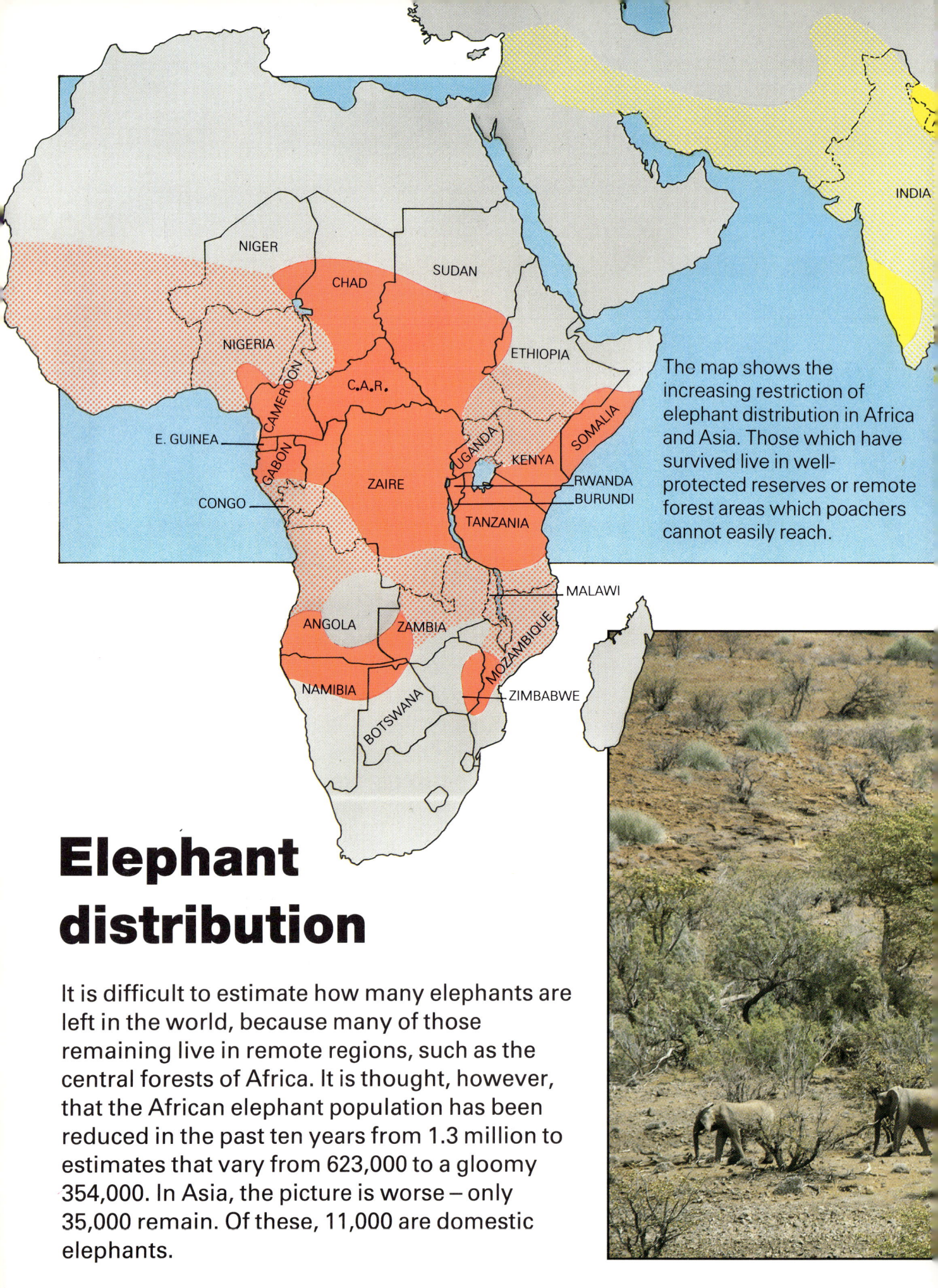

The map shows the increasing restriction of elephant distribution in Africa and Asia. Those which have survived live in well-protected reserves or remote forest areas which poachers cannot easily reach.

Elephant distribution

It is difficult to estimate how many elephants are left in the world, because many of those remaining live in remote regions, such as the central forests of Africa. It is thought, however, that the African elephant population has been reduced in the past ten years from 1.3 million to estimates that vary from 623,000 to a gloomy 354,000. In Asia, the picture is worse – only 35,000 remain. Of these, 11,000 are domestic elephants.

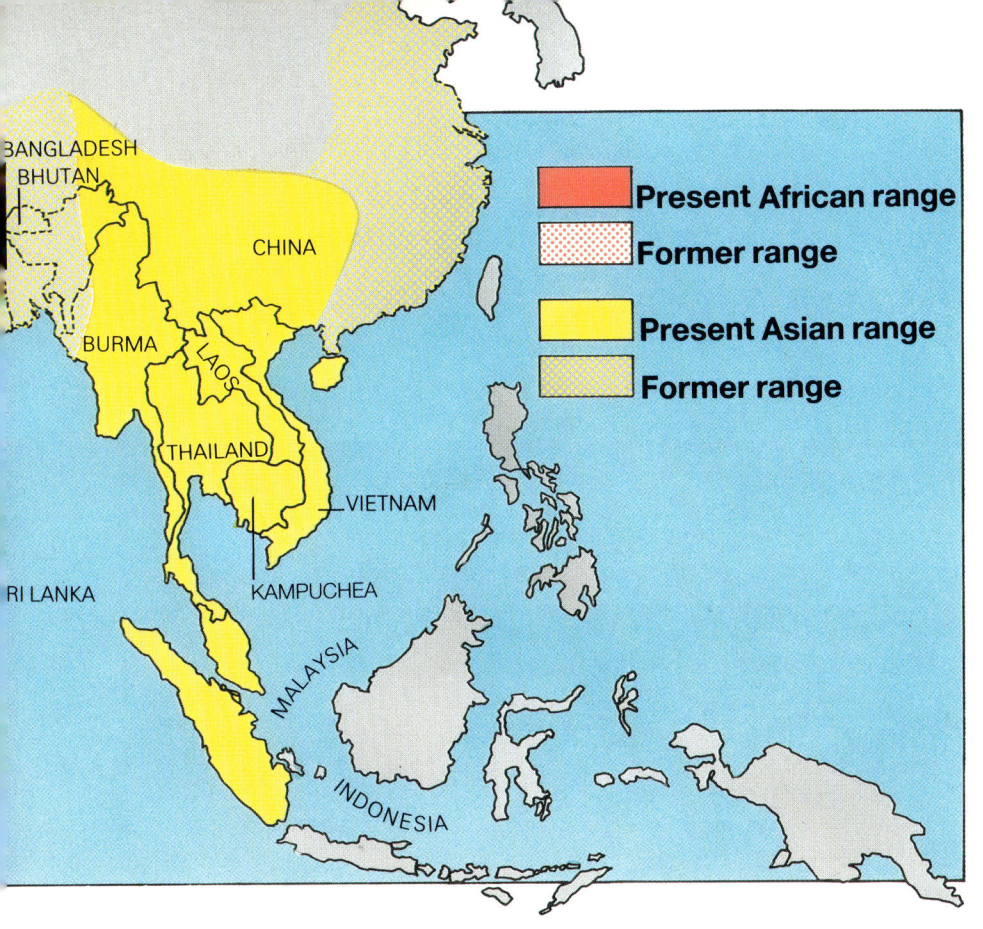

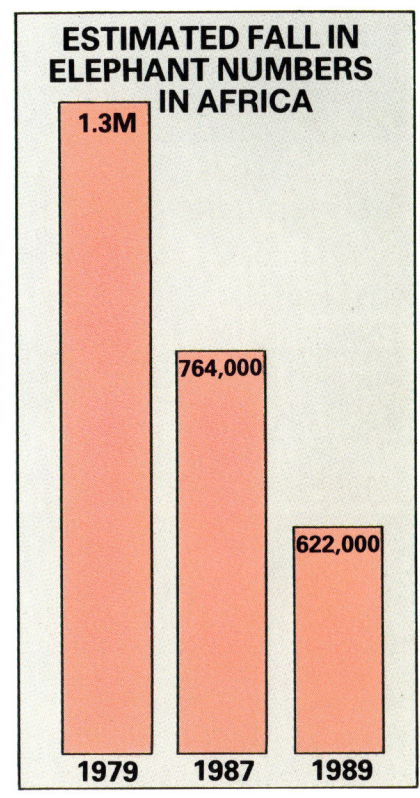

■ (red)	Present African range
■ (dotted)	Former range
■ (yellow)	Present Asian range
■ (pale yellow)	Former range

ESTIMATED FALL IN ELEPHANT NUMBERS IN AFRICA

- 1979: 1.3M
- 1987: 764,000
- 1989: 622,000

◁ This herd of elephants is following the dried-up Uniab River, in Damaraland, Namibia.

△ The absence of elephant surveys means that nobody knows how many elephants survive in Namibia.

Asian elephants once lived in a vast area that stretched from the lowland coastal forests to the Himalayan foothills. They were distributed in a belt that runs south of the Himalayas across Asia from Iraq to northern China. Today, isolated populations survive in forested hilly country in northern India, Sri Lanka, parts of Indochina, Malaysia, Indonesia and southern China.

Some African elephants live on the savannah, while others live in forests. They were once widespread across Africa, south of the Sahara. Today, this is no longer the case. Large herds still remain in Zimbabwe and South Africa, but in Uganda and Kenya they are slowly disappearing. Only two percent of the African elephant's range receives adequate protection. If poaching pressure continues, even these elephants will be at risk.

The slaughter

Elephants are poached only for their tusks. The meat is not usually taken and carcasses are left to rot. This wasteful slaughter reached a peak in the 1970s, when the value of ivory rose and the illegal hunting of elephants increased dramatically.

In the 1960s, ivory was bought from local hunters for about 45 cents a pound. In the 1970s the price went up to six dollars a pound. In Kenya, the impact of this increased demand was tragic. The country lost over half its elephants in seven years. Elsewhere, the situation was even worse. During the years of Idi Amin's rule in Uganda, nine out of ten elephants were killed.

In recent years, Africa has seen many violent wars with increasingly modernized armies. Consequently, more guns have been brought into the continent. This has meant that more semi-automatic and automatic weapons have been made available for commercial poachers.

During the 1980s, it is thought that between 50,000 and 150,000 elephants were killed each year. Most were taken from places where law enforcement was weak and poachers had easy access to reserves. But nowadays, more elephants must die to satisfy the trade.

The large, mature bulls, called "tuskers," have been mostly wiped out and so poachers must turn to increasingly younger elephants with smaller tusks. In 1979, tusk size averaged 22lbs (9.8kg). This meant that 51 elephants had to be killed for every ton of ivory. In 1987, average tusk size was 10lbs (4.7kg), which meant that 106 elephants died for every ton of ivory.

> "Suddenly this summer, disaster has hit African elephants. Ivory poachers have stepped up their attacks to a point where, unless drastic action is taken quickly, the species could become extinct within ten years... Yet another species wiped out by the ruthless greed of man; and that, the greatest species of them all."
>
> **Elspeth Huxley, author of *The Flame Trees of Thika***

◁ Poachers from Somalia kill the most elephants. They will even kill people who try to stop them.

△ In many parts of Kenya today, scenes like this are proof of the continued killing of elephants.

The ivory trade

The ivory trade is not new. In the past it was lawful and relied on legally acquired tusks. Animals die of old age or disease, or are shot by park rangers to control populations in the reserves. In the past, elephants were hunted for sport. All dead mature elephants leave ivory, and this was sold to the ivory workshops of the Far East to be turned into ornaments and jewelry.

Today, it is thought that 20 percent of Hong Kong's ivory comes from natural deaths and controlled shooting. This means that more than half – 80 percent – of the ivory comes from illegal killings.

▽ The Hong Kong ivory carver (below) prefers the straight tusks of African forest elephants, found in west and central Africa.

The export of ivory from Zaire is against the law, and so most of Hong Kong's forest elephant tusks must have been acquired illegally.

The ivory trade involves many countries and each plays a different role. Producer countries, like Kenya and Zaire, supply the elephants. Smuggler countries, like Sudan and Burundi, issue false papers to "legalize" and ship out illegal ivory from neighboring countries. Converter countries, like Hong Kong and Singapore, convert teeth into trinkets; and consumer countries, like Japan, India, the United States and those in the European Community (EC), buy the ivory products. India used to depend on the Asian elephant for its ivory jewelry, but now imports ivory from Africa. At each stage in the ivory trade chain, it is difficult to recognize lawful from poached ivory and so the movement of raw ivory is rarely checked. In a store, it would be difficult to know if the product on sale was made from legal or illegal ivory.

Several countries are stockpiling ivory as protection against the time when elephants become extinct. Burundi is sitting on 100 tons, all of which must be illegal because Burundi has no elephants!

▽ Raw ivory can be bought over the counter (below). More people are hoarding ivory, both legal and illegal, as an insurance against a slump in the world money markets. About 600 tons is stockpiled in Hong Kong.

Between 1,000,000 and 100,000 hectares

Less than 100,000 hectares

Information not available

Habitat destruction

The greatest threat to the survival of the Asian elephant is the destruction of its living space. Forests throughout southern Asia are being cleared by logging companies to produce cheap hardwoods, and by farmers to grow crops for the third world. Elephants are confined to isolated forest patches which are situated between vast areas of farm land. Inevitably, elephants and farmers come into conflict, and elephants which have become a nuisance are killed.

△ The map above shows how the destruction of tropical forest has led to the loss of elephant living space.

▽ The stripping of entire hillsides (below) has deprived the elephant of its habitat.

△ Deprived of its natural food, an elephant finds an easy meal at a garbage dump. In Rwanda, the government had most of the elephants killed. There was no space for them to live. In West Africa, the destruction of dense forest areas in which it was difficult for poachers to operate, is causing the decline in elephant numbers.

Over a century ago, Africa had 10 million elephants and only 16 million people. Today, there are over 500 million people. Their need for land has confined the surviving elephants to a quarter of their former range. Every 25-30 years, the human population south of the Sahara doubles and the pressure on Africa's land increases. Each year, since 1950, African elephants have been losing about two percent of their habitat, and each year there are 20 percent fewer elephants.

Anti-poaching

"We are lacking in resources to do our job. We have few vehicles, no radio and 21 mostly ageing guns for 55 men. Poachers have killed 50 elephants in the last ten years. Now, instead of the older bulls with bigger tusks, they are killing whatever they can."

**Johannes Balozi
Warden-in-charge,
Mikumi National Park,
Tanzania.**

◁ These national park rangers on anti-poaching patrol must be constantly on their guard. The poachers are often highly organized and carry modern machine guns. It would be easy for the patrol to fall into a trap. Poachers would not hesitate to kill the rangers as well as the elephants.

▽ The inset photograph shows the headquarters of the anti-poaching rangers that guard the Masai Mara Reserve, Kenya.

▽ In national parks and game reserves, wild animals have the right of way. Traffic must stop for elephants. The animals ignore automobiles since they are used to seeing the many tourist buses.

Several African national parks were set up to conserve elephants – Tsavo and Amoseli in Kenya, Hwange in Zimbabwe and Kruger in South Africa. Not all these parks, however, are successful in protecting their elephants. Only those with strong anti-poaching units have managed to stop the poachers. In Zimbabwe, the elite 1st Parachute Regiment has been enlisted to try and guard the elephants and capture the poachers who cross the border from Mozambique. So far, the strategy has worked and Zimbabwe's elephants are doing well.

In Kenya, however, there has been a sadder story. Somali poachers, known locally as "shiftas," have slaughtered elephant herds. But the Kenyan government is taking the conservation of their remaining elephants more seriously, and British army advisers are training a crackdown squad of 60 Kenyan gamekeepers to reinforce existing anti-poaching units. It is hoped that such measures will protect the elephants from eventual extinction.

Research

In 1976, scientists were beginning to realize that elephants in Africa were in danger and the first detailed survey was undertaken. Elephants are counted from light aircraft, which fly five miles apart, in straight lines about 350 feet above the ground. Savannah elephants in the open are easy to see, but the forest elephants are hidden by the trees.

Research on such a grand scale can be vague and so other methods are sought. Today, scientists in rough terrain vehicles follow herds and observe behavior at close range. Each elephant has its own distinct features, which can be recorded in a photographic log.

The close study of elephant groups has shown how disruptive the removal of the older, mature individuals can be. These are the ones with the largest tusks and are most likely to be killed by poachers. It has been found that the removal of a large male "tusker" from elephant society can severely affect breeding patterns.

▽ Elephants are stunned with a dart containing a sleeping drug (below left). While drugged, they are fitted with a radio collar (below). This transmits a signal that enables a scientist to follow at a distance.

Radio tracking has revealed much about elephant life. Already, it has shown that a family unit is not alone, but is part of a bigger elephant "clan" along with other related families. This kind of discovery will allow scientists to develop plans that will enable the surviving elephants to live in the space available to them.

Space to survive

Reserves must be large in order to provide elephants with the amount of space and food that they need. With humans increasingly taking over elephant living space, a clash between the two is perhaps inevitable. Scientists and national park administrators must therefore find ways by which elephants and people can coexist.

In Malaysia, where space is limited, elephants are kept away from oil palm plantations by electric fences. In Sri Lanka, they are being moved to areas where they can roam with more freedom. In central India, attempts have been made to connect three of the reserves which were once part of the ancient home range of the local elephant herds. Similarly, in northeastern India, it has been suggested that a corridor of protected forest in the Himalayan foothills runs from India to Bhutan, to create the largest reserve for the Asian elephant.

△ Elephants like to eat tree bark. In well-protected reserves, large numbers of elephants can outgrow the living space and cause considerable damage to the vegetation. What therefore should be done about too many elephants?

In Sumatra, "rogue" elephants that have been damaging crops are being moved to larger reserves. The park rangers have enlisted the help of trained Thai elephants, which lead the wild elephants away from cultivated areas.

In Zimbabwe and South Africa, conservation measures have been so successful there are more elephants than the parks can support. Rather than let elephants die of hunger the decision was taken to "cull" the surplus.

In Zimbabwe, the local people benefit from this method of killing. The ivory is traded legally, the meat sold in local markets, the skin made into leather, and the fat turned into cooking oil.

In South Africa, surplus young animals are drugged with darts fired from helicopters and shipped to zoos and wildlife parks all over the world. Although it may seem cold-blooded, these measures have allowed the elephant to survive.

△ The decision to cull elephants is not taken lightly. Park management plans, based on the latest research findings, are carefully considered in order to determine whether a herd should live or die. In 1983, for example, a severe drought devastated Kenya's Tsavo National Park. There was very little water or food available. It was decided to kill some of the dying elephants so that the stronger ones could survive the harsh conditions.

Stop the trade

The most important organization involved in the control of the ivory trade is the Convention on Trade in Endangered Species (CITES). It is an international forum which decides whether an animal or parts of an animal can be traded commercially.

Most of the 103 member nations of CITES would like a total ban on the ivory trade, while those countries with a surplus of elephants still want to trade in legal ivory. Many countries, including the United States, Switzerland, and those in the E.C. have introduced restrictions to ban the import of raw ivory.

Nevertheless, illegal ivory shipments still get through. Even officials at London's Heathrow Airport have been deceived and have mistakenly issued legal papers to accompany poached ivory destined for Hong Kong.

Countries with large stocks want to trade their ivory, and indeed, the CITES ivory monitoring unit is itself partly funded from the selling of this ivory. This will encourage the trade, and as long as there is a demand for ivory, elephants will be unlawfully killed.

▽ One of the greatest problems in controlling the trade in ivory is the stockpiles of tusks, like those shown below, which are stored all over the world. Some are from legal culling or natural deaths, but most have been confiscated from poachers.

△ Richard Leakey (left), Kenya's Director of Wildlife, recommended that the country's stockpile of seized ivory should be destroyed, not sold. He realized that this was one way to draw world attention to the plight of elephants. President Moi of Kenya ordered the tusks to be burned in public.

◁ The elephant has always been looked upon with great awe and wonderment, and is often featured in religious stories, legends and folklore. Asian elephants still play an important role in traditional religious ceremonies throughout southern Asia. This "temple tusker" (left) is dressed in expensive robes, and carries a golden casket containing an ancient religious relic.

Captive elephants

Throughout history, elephants have been used in the service of man. There is evidence of elephants being used as beasts of burden over 5,500 years ago in the Indus Valley. The elephant's great strength and endurance have meant that they have been used in warfare, agriculture and forestry. Their natural gentleness and dignity have lead to their use in ceremonies. The Asian elephant has mostly been taken into captivity, as it is more docile than the African.

The latest elephant to serve the Temple of the Tooth and carry the ancient Buddhist relic through the streets of Kandy in Sri Lanka, was carried there by air in a US transport plane from Thailand. The 11 year-old tusker was trained for two years to take part in the procession.

△ These captive Asian elephants are trained to move tree trunks in logging camps. Elephants are able to work in areas where vehicles would be unsuitable. In Zaire, a few African elephants have been trained to move logs. It is ironic that these animals are helping to destroy the forest in which their wild relatives once lived.

There are many arguments relating to the keeping of elephants in zoos or as working animals. Some people feel they are too big and should be left to live a natural life in the wild. Others stress the importance of breeding elephants in captivity. If successful, this process could serve as an insurance measure against them becoming extinct in the wild.

It was thought at one time that the breeding of captive working animals would help in the conservation of the Asian elephant. But down the centuries, very few logging elephants have been bred in captivity. In fact, the population of domestic elephants in Thailand has dropped from over 13,000 in 1950 to less than 5,000 in 1982.

Today, new recruits are often captured and traded illegally. They are taken from isolated wild herds in Thailand, Burma and war-torn Kampuchea and Laos. It is hoped that the introduction of stricter controls will keep closer checks on captive elephants.

▷ This picture of a mother elephant and her baby in a zoo is rare. Elephants are difficult to breed in captivity. The problem is that bull elephants can be very dangerous and are not suited to living in a zoo. With few male elephants, the possibility of breeding is greatly reduced. Therefore, some of the young elephants seen in zoos will not have been bred in the zoo, but taken from the wild.

The future

The long term future for the elephant looks bleak. Despite international concern and effort, the numbers of both African and Asian elephants have declined. There are only a few herds remaining in a handful of protected national parks. The rest are living in isolated refuges, which are safe because they are remote and not inhabited. The African forest elephants can live unharmed as long as their forests are not cut down and poachers cannot reach them.

But the human population across southern Asia and throughout Africa is rapidly expanding. It is demanding, and indeed taking, more and more space in which to live and cultivate crops. The wilderness areas are shrinking, and, as they disappear, the elephants will have very few places in which to live.

Also, while ivory continues to be valuable, there will always be people ready to kill elephants solely for their tusks. If these trends continue, elephants will only be seen behind large steel fences in well-guarded reserves.

"Until now, the conservation community has been frustrated by lack of hard data about the ivory trade and its impact on the survival of the African elephant. The new Ivory Trade Review Group report makes it clear, however, that we face a conservation crisis without parallel."

Russell Train Chairman, World Wildlife Fund, United States.

▽ A herd of African elephants, walking one behind the other across the savannah, is becoming an increasingly rare sight. If the moves to stem the trade in ivory are not successful, and the wild places in which elephants live are not conserved, the species could become extinct within the next 20 years.

There are, however, a few signs that things could change. Many countries have announced plans to ban the ivory trade. If ivory ceased to be valuable, then nobody would want to hoard it. And nobody would want to kill elephants.

In addition, some countries, like Kenya, are spending more money on protecting their surviving elephants from poachers. If these trends continue then the elephant's chances of survival will improve.

△ Countries with elephants have realized that they are big business – not for the tusks, but because they attract tourists. In addition, many African and Asian countries which depend on forestry rather than tourism, will suffer in the future if elephants do not survive to disperse the seeds of the forest trees.

Elephant fact file 1

Largest Recorded Bull
Largest Recorded Cow

400 cms
350
300
250
200
150
100
50

10 years to maturity
5-10 years
2-5 years
0-2 years

The largest known elephant was a bull African elephant killed in Angola in 1955. It weighed 12.25 tons and stood 13 feet at the shoulder. One tusk was broken but the other was 8 feet long. They weighed 165lbs.

Size and Differences

African savannah elephants are larger than their forest relatives and Asian elephants. African bulls stand about 10 feet at the shoulder and weigh 5.25 tons. Asian bulls stand 9 feet at the shoulder and weigh 4.5 tons.

In addition to size, there are several other differences between African and Asian elephants. The African elephant has much larger ears, and the highest point of its body is its back. The Asian elephant has slightly smaller ears and the highest part is the head.

The African has longer legs and a more slender body. Both African bulls and cows have tusks, while only Asian bulls have tusks.

Both types of elephant have large, padded feet. This distributes the huge weight of the elephant over a large area, and means that elephants leave very little imprint.

African

Asian

Distinctive Features

The large flapping ears of the elephant act like a pair of radiators. They allow the animal to cool down when the weather is hot. The ears are lined with blood vessels from which body heat can escape, thus preventing the animal from overheating.

African elephants, living on the hot, open savannahs, have the largest ears. The wrinkly skin traps and retains water to help keep the animal cool.

The tusks, which start to grow from the age of two and continue throughout life, have several functions. The largest tusks are carried by the strongest elephants. They can be used to peel off tree bark, or dig up roots, or even in fighting displays.

Trunks

The elephant cannot lower its massive head, so it developed the trunk. The trunk is incredibly strong – it can carry a tree trunk – and is very sensitive – it can pick up a leaf. The African elephant has two finger like projections at the end of the trunk while the Asian has one.

The trunk has many uses. It picks up food and sucks up water. It can act as a snorkel when swimming. It can suck up and squirt mud or dust over the body. It is used in greetings and as an amplifier for loud calls. And, it can smell the air to detect danger.

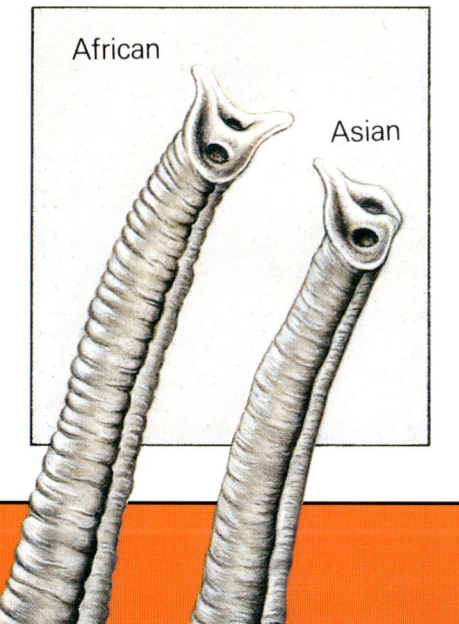

African

Asian

Elephant fact file 2

Range

Elephants are very large animals, so they need an ample home range in which to look for food and water and find shade during the hottest parts of the day.

African elephants need 300 sq miles if food and water is plentiful, but 550 sq miles if conditions are poor. They can walk for long distances, at about 3 miles per hour, and travel 18 miles nonstop in order to find food. Journeys made both by African and Asian elephants tend to follow the same routes, resulting in well-worn "elephant roads."

Herds

Elephant herds consist mainly of closely related adult cows – mothers, daughters and sisters – and their young offspring. When females grow up they stay with the herd and breed. When a herd or family unit becomes too large, subunits break away and new herds are formed. In this way, several family herds will be related and be part of a large "clan." Young bulls leave the herd when they mature and live separately.

The head of the herd is the oldest cow, the matriarch. She is usually the largest animal. She makes all the decisions. The rest of the herd works under her guidance. At about 50 years of age she stops breeding, but continues to be the leader.

Members of the herd communicate by using different senses – smell, vision, touch and sound. Most conversations are carried out with sounds which are made in the throat, and keep the herd in contact.

- Sire Bull
- Young Bulls
- Matriarch
- Adult sisters/daughters
- Juveniles and sub-adults
- Infants

28

Elephants need a lot of food and water. An adult requires about 335lbs of food a day and 24 gallons of water. The food is crunched by just four huge molar teeth — one on each side in the top and bottom of each jaw. As they wear out, five more sets can grow to replace them. When all six sets are worn out, the elephant dies.

Food
African savannah elephants eat grass, leaves, flowers and fruits during the productive rainy season. Only twigs, tree bark and branches are eaten when it is dry. The food travels rapidly through the gut.

Elephants are not ruminants like cows, but have a sac (the cecum) at the junction of the small and large intestines. Here, microbes break down the tough plant food.

Fact file 3

Mating

The elephant's reproductive cycle coincides with the weather. When the rains have come and the grass is lush, it takes a couple of months of good feeding before a female is ready to mate.

At the same time, a bull elephant undergoes dramatic changes in his body chemistry, known as "musth," which lasts for three months. The bull becomes more aggressive and sexually active. A gland on the side of the head secretes a fluid which runs down the face.

A female is in heat for just a few days. So, right across the home ranges of several herds, individual cows are in heat at different times.

The bulls must walk long distances between herds to find the receptive cows. Bulls, therefore, must be fit and strong, simply to do all the traveling.

On finding a cow ready to mate, a bull is probably not the only suitor. He must drive off his rivals for the right to mate with her. The giants push and shove with their heads and interlock trunks and tusks.

Mating takes place when the bull mounts the cow. Immature bulls will often try to copy their larger relatives. The females shun them. The end of the mating season is often heralded by fleeing cows pursued by noisy young bulls.

> The gestation period for elephants is about 22 months. Birth is timed to coincide with the wet season. This ensures the mother is feeding well when the baby needs milk. Baby African elephants are 264lbs at birth; Asian elephants are 220lbs.

Dummy Charge

Mothers and Babies
Cooperation between the rest of the herd is important in the early life of a baby elephant. At the birth, the mature cows gather around and help the mother. One might take away the fetal membrane while another will help the newborn calf to its feet.

The idea of a family unit is instilled in a youngster right from the start of its life. The baby suckles for up to four years from a pair of breasts between the mother's front legs.

At 15 years old, the young elephant's growth rate slows, although bulls experience a spurt of growth between 20-30 years old. It is at this stage that they grow larger than the females.

The early life of both cows and bulls is spent under the protection of the herd. If danger threatens, the mature cows form a protective group around the calves. The matriarch alone steps forward to confront the threat. If one of the herd is injured the rest will come to its help.

Charging
The usual elephant response to danger is to stand fast. The sheer size of a matriarch is enough to deter any potential attacker (except, that is, one with a gun).

If the threat does not go away the matriarch will charge. She runs forward, spreads out her ears for maximum effect, raises her trunk, and trumpets loudly. If this mock charge fails, she will either attack and trample the foe or, if the threat is too unusual, turn and run with the rest of the herd.

Index

A
African elephant 5, 6, 7, 10, 13, 16, 22, 23, 26
Amin, Idi 8
anti-poaching units 14, 15
Asian elephant 5, 6, 7, 11, 12, 18, 22, 23, 26

B
ban on trade 20, 25
Bhutan 18
breeding 16, 23, 30
bull elephant 23, 28, 30
Burma 23
Burundi 11

C
captivity 22, 23
charging 31
China 7
CITES 20
close study 16
controlled shooting 10
"converter countries" 11
cows 28, 30, 31
culling 19, 20

D
distribution 6, 7
domestic elephants 6, 18, 22, 23

E
EC 11, 20
"elephant roads" 28

F
family units 17, 28, 31
farming 12, 18, 24
food 12, 13, 18, 19, 27-29
forest 6, 7, 12, 13, 16, 18, 23-25

G
guns 8, 15

H
habitat destruction 12, 13
herds 28, 31
Himalayas 7
Hong Kong 10, 11, 20
human population 13, 18, 24

I
India 7, 11, 18
Indonesia 7
Iraq 7
ivory 5, 8-10, 19-21, 25
ivory products 10, 11
Ivory Task Force 20
ivory trade 5, 10, 11, 20, 21, 24, 25

J
Japan 11

K
Kenya 7-9, 11, 15, 19, 21, 25

L
Laos 23
Leakey, Richard 21
life expectancy 31

M
Malaysia 7, 18
mammoths 5
mating 30
meat 5, 8, 19
"musth" 30

N
Namibia 7
national parks 15, 18, 24
natural death 10, 20

O
overpopulation 19, 20

P
poachers 6-9, 13-16, 20, 24, 25
population 5-7, 13
price of ivory 5, 8, 9
protection 7, 9, 15, 25

R
radio-tracking 17
range 28
rangers 10, 15, 18
religion 22
research 16, 17, 19
reserves 6, 9, 10, 14, 15, 18, 24
Rwanda 13

S
Singapore 11
size 26
"smuggler countries" 11
Somalia 9, 15
South Africa 7, 15, 19
sport 10
Sri Lanka 7, 18
stockpiling 11, 20, 21
Sumatra 18
surveys 7, 16
Switzerland 20

T
Thailand 23
tourism 15, 25
trunks 27
"tuskers" 9, 16, 22
tusks 5, 8-10, 16, 24, 25, 27

U
Uganda 7, 8
United States 11, 20

Y
young elephants 9, 31

Z
Zaire 10, 11, 23
Zimbabwe 7, 15, 19
zoos 19, 23

Photographic Credits:
Cover and pages 4-5, 6-7, 9, 10l, 13, 18, 21 inset, 24-25, 27, 28, 30 and 31: Bruce Coleman Ltd; pages 8, 10r, 11, 19, 20 and 29: Rex Features; pages 12, 16 and 22: Survival Anglia; pages 14 and inset, 15, 21, 22-23 and 25: Planet Earth; page 17: Oxford Scientific Films; page 23: Paul Ross Photography.